Pleasing God and Manifesting Miracles

Rev Franklin N Abazie

Pleasing God and Manifesting Miracles

Copyright © 2014 by Rev Franklin N Abazie

All rights reserved. This book or any portion thereof may not be reproduced or used in any manner whatsoever without the express written permission of the publisher, except for the use of brief quotations in a book review. All Bible quotes are from King James Version and others as noted.

Published by: **F N Abazie Publishing House**
   a.k.a *Empowerment Bookstore*

Psalms 26:7 - That I may publish with the voice of thanksgiving, and tell of all thy wondrous works.

To order additional copies, wholesale or bookings:
Church Office: (973) 372-7518
33 Schley Street • Newark, NJ 07112
email: pastorfranknto@yahoo.com

   www.fnabaziepublishinghouse.org

   www.fnabaziehealingministries.org

Cover Design: www.AngelPrints.net

First Printing, 2014 in the USA
   by Whole Without A Crack Publications

Dedication

I thank God for His is constant mercy and sufficient grace upon my life.

I thank all of my Spiritual mentors in the faith; mentors that delivered my life from the hand of the tormentor.

I give thanks to God for my wife and my three children for their family support.

I give special thanks to Bishop David Oyedepo, for the word of God through him that has influenced my life.

I give special thanks to late Arch Bishop Benson Idahosa, the late Kenneth Hagin and the late Oral Robert of blessed memory.

www.WWACPSelfPublishing.net

Table of Content

Introduction ... 3

Chapter 1 ... 7
The Mystery of Frustration

Chapter 2 ... 17
The Blessing of Faith

Chapter 3 ... 25
The Law of Faith

Chapter 4 ... 39
Understanding the Power of Winning Faith

Chapter 5 ... 45
Understanding Invisible Barriers

About the Author ... 51

Introduction

I recommend you do not to stagger concerning the promises of God through your unbelief, but be strong in faith, giving glory to God for faithful is He that called you, who also will do it. This book has been written to shatter and destroy every appearance of fear, doubt and unbelief inside of you. Jesus said "***do not be afraid, but only believe***" (Mark 5:36). This material has been written for your encouragement, establishment and blessing. 2 Timothy 2:9 says that the word of God is not bound. Therefore wherever you may find yourself, and find this book in your possession, take advantage of this book. For He sent His word and great is the company of them that publish it. If you commit yourself and be faithful in that which is least, He will make you faithful in that which is much.

I have written this book because "***Faith comes by hearing and hearing by the word of God***" (Romans 10:17). God wants you to be able to see the invisible, believe the impossible and do the incredible.

John 11:40

Introduction Cont'd

"Jesus said unto her, Said I not unto thee, that if thou wouldest believe, thou shouldest see the glory of God."
Paraphrased by me: "If you believe you shall see the glory of God."

The Outcome of Faith is the result of faith. It practically shows, without any doubt, the result of faith. Until you take the written word into the tablet of your heart, you are not fit for the supernatural in the kingdom of God. I therefore admonish and encourage you, in the way of the Lord, to accept this book without any reservation, doubt, fear or unbelief, but with a pure conscience; holding the mystery of faith that He who has promised is able to perform. With the help of this book, your faith will be built.

CHAPTER 1

The Mystery of Frustration

"Looking diligently lest any man fail of the grace of God; lest any root of bitterness springing up trouble you and thereby many be defiled."

~ Hebrew 12:15

Frustration is a weapon of the enemy to steal your joy and take away the grace of God upon your life. It is an agenda of the enemy to defile you. Frustration is a device of the devil to depress you, keep you stagnant and in bitterness. I prophesy into your life that frustration shall not have dominion over you any more, in the name of Jesus, Amen!

God has a solid plan and purpose for your life and the enemy also has his devices. Satan wants to hide your purpose from you, steal your blessings and keep you in perpetual darkness. This book will reveal the hidden mysteries manifesting frustration over your life; it will expose all of the devices and weapons the enemy has used over the years to keep you in the wilderness of sickness, torment, fear and depression. The Holy Spirit will use this book to conquer all satanic plans, demonic gang ups, disgrace satanic mafias and totally expose the enemy of your progress. Have you ever been angry and frustrated before? Ecclesiastes 7:9 says, ***"Be not hasty in thy spirit to be angry; for anger resteth in the bosom of fools."*** Anger is a product of frustration.

I declare the mighty hand of God upon you, in the name of Jesus. You must be released from opposition, from contention and marital bondage, in the name of Jesus, Amen!

Have you ever been frustrated in what you want to do in life? W. Clement Stone said, "Tell everyone what you want to do and someone will help you do it." Are you restricted and frustrated from doing the will of God for your life? W. Clement Stone said: "You are a product of your environment." These are some of the principles and fundamentals needed to terminate frustration before it graduates and matures.

The psychologists say that **frustration** is a response to opposition and contention. It is greatly related to stress and confusion. Frustration arises from the perceived resistance to the fulfillment of an individual's plan (Jeremiah 29:11). The greater the obstruction, and the greater the will. Spiritually, frustration is lack of faith and trust in God. It is the result of attempting to do something in our your strength.

Frustration may be internal or external. In many people, internal frustration may arise from challenges in fulfillment and instinctual drives and needs, or dealing with perception. A lack of social situations can also be an internal source of frustration; when one has goals that interfere with one another, it can create feelings of frustration. External causes of frustration involve conditions outside an individual, such as a blocked road or a difficult task. While coping with frustration, some individuals may engage in passive aggressive behavior, thus making it difficult to identify the original cause of their frustration, as the responses are indirect. A more direct, and common response, is a propensity towards aggression.

Deuteronomy 2:3 says, ***"Ye have compassed this mountain long enough; turn you northward."***

Frustration is a mystery that cannot be understood in the energy of the flesh. It is a demonic device to terminate your future. It is reasonable to be at a location for a while, but if you have been in a particular location for a very long time you will begin to be agitated, worried and stressed out. Deuteronomy 2:3 says, ***"Ye have compassed this mountain long enough; turn you northward."*** It is inevitable that you will pretend all is well when the spirit of frustration has taken hold of you. Daniel was frustrated into the lion's den (Daniel 6:22). Joseph was frustrated in a pit and in a slavery prison (Genesis 37:20, Genesis 39:5). David was frustrated in the bush. Paul was stoned and frustrated in prison. Jesus was never frustrated, not even on the cross blotting out the hand writing of ordinances that was against us, which was contrary to us Jesus took it out of the way nailing it to his cross, and having spoiled principalities and powers He made a show of them openly, triumphing over them in it. Frustration comes in different versions, fashions and forms. It is interesting to note, however, that someone can be frustrated without knowing it.

I come against hindering spirits, in the name of Jesus. Are you frustrated? Receive the grace of God, in the name of Jesus, Amen! In 1 Corinthians 16:9, the scripture says ***"For a great door and effectual is opened unto me, and there are many adversaries."*** Proverbs 24:4 warns: ***"…cease from*** *thine own wisdom."* It is a noble choice to have a plan and a purpose for your life. It is even more rewarding to have a goal, a mission and a vision, but until you discover God's solemn gift and calling over your life, your plans and ideas will remain in frustration. The scripture says that your gift will make room for you and your gift will bring you before great men (Proverbs 18:16, Romans 11:29). The gift and calling of God is without repentance Therefore, to avoid frustration, learn to commit your ways unto the Lord, trust also in Him and he shall bring it to pass. There are many plans you can come up with in your life, but only the counsel of the Lord shall stand (Proverbs 19:21). There are many sources of frustration in life. Let us take a look at a few:

1. ***Environmental Frustration:*** This type of frustration has ravaged most third world countries to a despondent degree that the average citizen would rather be an economical and financial slave in Europe, Canada and America than be a victim of despair in their own country. This type of frustration is predominant in Nigeria where princes want to work as servants. Ecclesiastes 10:8 says, *"I have seen servants upon horses and princes walking as servants upon the earth."* This type of frustration has promoted the gospel of Prosper-

ity. This is the type of frustration that is causing a mass influx in most Pentecostal ministries, resulting in mega churches, in West Africa, Nigeria in particular. God blesses the work of your hand. God has given us wisdom to plan and succeed in life. Although most Pastors have taken advantage of environmental frustration by preaching the gospel of giving and receiving miracles, the center focus should be on grace and truth, and the love of Jesus Christ. The scripture teaches us in Ecclesiastes 10:10: *"..but wisdom is profitable to direct."* Environmental frustration has affected the way people think, believe and act. Proverb 23:7 says, *"For as he thinketh in his heart, so is he."* Political and economic instability is a major cause of environmental frustration. Other promoting factors are tribal wars and civil wars, coup d'état. W. Clement Stone said, "You are a product of your environment." On the other side, a more regimental restricted society, with unfavorable laws, is also an environmental frustration. W. Clement Stone said "You are a product of your environment. Choose the environment that will best develop you toward your objective. Analyze your life in terms of its environment. Are the things around you helping you toward success or are they holding you back?" Unfavorable environment is a primary factor that causes frustration. I pray that your eyes be opened to the truth, in Jesus' name, and that you will be free from any form of environmental frustration, in Jesus' name, Amen.

2. ***Personal Frustration:*** There are short comings, unforeseen circumstances and uncertainties that will inevitably cause personal frustration. Despite this, if you can trust God, commit your ways to Him, be persistent, consistent and diligent, God will surely bring you victory. Proverb 23:18 says, ***"For surely there is an end and thine expectation shall not be cut off."*** The cure to personal frustration is consistent, persistent, and diligent dedication, and commitment in a disciplined manner. Habakkuk 2:3 says, ***"For the vision is for an appointed time, but at the end it shall speak and not lie, though it tarry, wait for it because it will surely come. It will not tarry."*** We are all created with some amount of personal desire, expectation, aspirations and goals. There are financial challenges, obstacles and limitations, family backgrounds and academic limitations that will cause anyone to be shy away, dwarf and handicap when it comes to accomplishing their goals. It can also make them short of reaching their expectations. No one can fulfill all of their wants and expectations in life at one time. One great man said that "life is in phases and Men in sizes." At any phase

of life, you must leearn to be content and give thanks and glory unto the name of the Lord. Ingratitude and ungratefulness are the reason for personal frustration. Murmuring and complaining will lead you from frustration to depression. I urge you today to make up your mind and thank God for His grace upon your life. Renew your mind and begin a new life of thanksgiving and appreciation to God. What has happened, you know, what would have happened, you do not know; what will happen when you begin to give thanks to God is far greater than a lifetime of loses! Personal frustration must be destroyed in your life this time, in Jesus' name. You will not die in despair and despondency. Ecclesiastes 9:4 says, ***"To whom that is joined to all the living there is hope; For a living dog is better than a dead lion."***

3. ***Conflicting Frustration:*** This type of frustration results when anyone depends on someone else or a company for a source of income and livelihood. Conflicting frustration results from arising conflict between employee and employer. Such conflicts create psychological pressure for the workers. Gradually, such psychological pressure and gloominess turns into frustration. We are created to be kings and priests on the earth (Revelation 5:10) not servants and peasants. I pray

that God visits you in your hour of need and makes you an employer of labor, in Jesus' name.

4. ***Motivational frustration:*** Paul said, in 1 Corinthians 16:9, ***"for a great door and effectual is opened unto me, and there are many adversaries."*** I want you to know that the enemy is against your rising. This type of frustration is a result of obstacles, mountains and challenges. You can be motivated to follow the call of God upon your life and you can have the zeal of the Lord to do the work of God upon your life. When the vision, plan and purpose of God upon your life is stagnant, you become frustrated.

After carefully creating awareness of our upcoming crusade in Nigeria, I printed a flyer and called on some Pastors to be ready for it. The crusade was supposed to take place between October 17th – October 24, 2013. Thieves invaded my house on September 14th. Among the items stolen was my brief case, which contained my traveling documents. Although I was motivated to travel to Africa to preach the word of God, I was frustrated because the enemy that broke into my house disrupted my plans. I urge you to take all your plans and agendas to God; trust also in Him and He will make a way for you, in Jesus' Name.

CHAPTER 2

The Blessing of Faith

"Jesus said unto her, Said I not unto thee, that if thou wouldest believe, thou shouldest see the glory of God."

~ John 11:40

What is the Outcome of Faith?

The pre-requisite for faith to manifest in your life is your ability to believe in the unseen. 2 Corinthians 4:18 notes that, ***"while we look not at the things which are seen, but at the things which are not seen; For the things which are seen are temporal; but the things which are not seen are eternal."*** The Outcome of your faith is the result of your belief in the invisible, despite not being able to see it. It is your ability to capture the future through the practice of the scripture. Every scriptural word is loaded with exceeding great and precious promises that, by these, ye might be partakers of the divine nature, having escaped the corruption and frustration that is in the world through lust. The outcome of faith is the victory of faith. It is foolishness and ignorant to doubt the outcome of faith. Until you see faith in all you do, you are not a candidate of His blessings. Behind every successful man or woman in the kingdom of God, or in the secular world, is the result of faith. Jesus said, in Mark 9:23, *"...if thou canst believe, all things are possible to him that believeth."* The outcome of faith is believing God in the unseen to make good His promise. It is your ability to see the invisible, believe the incredible and do the impossible.

Faith is an expression of our confidence in God and the word of God. 1 John 5:14 notes: *"And this is the confidence we have in Him, that if we ask anything according to His will, He heareth us."* Faith is the evidence of your obedience to the word of God. It is the pillar upon which you will win in the race of life. 1 John 5:4 reiterates that *"For whatsoever is born of God overcometh the world; and this is the victory that overcometh the world, even our faith."*

What then is Faith? Faith is a living force to overcome the battles of life. In life, you are in a race. Until you begin to fight the fight of faith, then and only then can you begin to conquer the battles of life. Faith is a spiritual force that will determine your portion in the land of the living. What then is Faith? Hebrew 11:1-3 says, *"Now faith is the substance of things hoped for, the evidence of things not seen. For by it the elders obtained a good report. Through faith we under-*

stand that the worlds were framed by the word of God, so that things which are seen were not made of things which do appear." Faith is the spiritual force that will connect you into your inheritance. *"For without faith it is impossible to please God"* (Hebrew 11:6). *"By faith we live"* Habakkuk 2:4 and Romans 1:17. *"By faith ye stand"* (2 Corinthians 1:24). *"For we walk by faith"* (2 Corinthians 5:7). Faith is absolute trust and obedience in the validity of the word of God. It is the supernatural currency for physical transactions. You will never make a mark on earth until you begin your transactions by faith. Jeremiah 33:3 says, *"Call unto me and I will answer thee, and shew thee great and mighty things which thou knowest not."* If you are operating by faith, there is a sure reward in due season. The reward is the blessing of faith and that is why I called this book *The Outcome of Faith*.

God can deliver unto you a prophetic word, but if you do not war and work it out, that prophecy will be cut short and aborted. 1 Timothy 1:18 says, *"This charge I commit unto thee, son Timothy. According to the prophecies which went before thee, that thou by them mightest war a good warfare."* You can be born to be great a president or a medical doctor, but if you do not study and be disciplined it will not come to pass in your lifetime. Paul warn Timothy in 1 Timothy 6:20, *"O Timothy, keep that which is committed to thy*

trust, avoiding profane and vain babblings, and oppositions of science falsely called." In this race of life we wrestle not against flesh and blood, but against principalities, against powers, against the rulers of darkness of this world, against spiritual wickedness in high places. Therefore until you pick up the helmet of salvation and the shield of faith you will not defeat and quench the fiery darts of the wicked. Do not be afraid Jesus said in Mark 5:36, ***"but only believe."*** James 2:19 says, ***"the devil also believe but he trembled."***

The Outcome of faith has foundation in your obedience to the word of God. ***"Faith without works is dead"*** (James 2:20, 26). The gift of faith will give you power, the word of faith will give you divine guidance but the spirit of faith will release your inheritance. Jesus cursed the fig tree in Mark 11:13-14 because of the time of the fig tree was not yet. ***"It was therefore not new to Jesus who, when Peter called into remembrance and said the fig tree which thou cursed is withered away"*** (Mark 11:21). It is interesting to note that Jesus responded and said ***"Have Faith in God"*** (Mark 11:22). To have faith in God is to believe in the mystery of faith and the mystery of faith will result in: <u>The Outcome of Faith.</u>

D. L. Moody the great man of God of the blessed memory

once said, "Is there any reason why you should not have faith in God?" The scripture, in 1 Kings 8:56, teaches *"that there hath not failed one word of all His good promise, which He promise by the hand of Moses His servant."* There is no reason to doubt God's precious promises in His word. If you understand the Outcome of Faith, then Satan is not permitted to attack your faith anymore. Jesus prayed for Peter that his faith faileth not (Luke 22:32). Peter failed to understand the outcome of his faith. Abram understood the outcome of faith. The scripture says, *"so Abram departed as the Lord had spoken to him."* A faith filled man will abound with blessings. (Also see Genesis 13:1-2). Accepting spiritual responsibility is the key for the outcome of faith. God has done His part, wake up and begin to do your own portion, in life, by faith.

Hebrew 11:11-33
"Through faith also Sara herself received strength to conceive seed, and was delivered of a child when she was past age, because she judged him faithful who had promised. Therefore sprang there even of one, and him as good as dead, so many as the stars of the sky in multitude, and as the sand which is by the sea shore innumerable. These all died in faith, not having received the promises, but having seen them afar off, and were persuaded of them, and em-

braced them, and confessed that they were strangers and pilgrims on the earth. For they that say such things declare plainly that they seek a country. And truly, if they had been mindful of that country from whence they came out, they might have had opportunity to have returned. But now they desire a better country, that is, an heavenly: wherefore God is not ashamed to be called their God: for he hath prepared for them a city. By faith Abraham, when he was tried, offered up Isaac: and he that had received the promises offered up his only begotten son, Of whom it was said, That in Isaac shall thy seed be called: Accounting that God was able to raise him up, even from the dead; from whence also he received him in a figure. By faith Isaac blessed Jacob and Esau concerning things to come. By faith Jacob, when he was a dying, blessed both the sons of Joseph; and worshipped, leaning upon the top of his staff. By faith Joseph, when he died, made mention of the departing of the children of Israel; and gave commandment concerning his bones. By faith Joseph, when he died, made mention of the departing of the children of Israel; and gave commandment concerning his bones. By faith Moses, when he was born, was hid three months of his parents, because they saw he was a proper child; and they were not afraid of the king's commandment. By faith Moses, when he was come to years, refused to be called the son of Pharaoh's daughter; Choosing rather to suffer affliction with the people of God, than to enjoy the pleasures of sin for a season; Esteeming the reproach of Christ greater riches than the treasures in Egypt: for he had respect unto the recompense of the reward. By faith he forsook Egypt, not fearing the wrath of the king: for he endured, as seeing him who is invisible. Through faith he kept the passover, and the sprinkling of blood, lest he that destroyed the firstborn should touch them. By faith they passed through the Red sea as by dry land: which the Egyptians assaying to do were drowned. By faith the walls of Jericho fell down, after they were compassed about seven days. By faith the harlot Rahab perished not with them that believed not, when she had received the spies with peace. And what shall I more say? for the time would fail me to tell of Gedeon, and of Barak, and of Samson, and of Jephthae; of David also, and Samuel, and of the prophets: Who through faith subdued kingdoms, wrought righteousness, obtained promises, stopped the mouths of lions. Quenched the violence of fire, escaped the edge of the sword, out of weakness were made strong, waxed valiant in fight, turned to flight the armies of the aliens."

CHAPTER 3

The Law of Faith

...And calleth those things which be not as though they were...

...He staggard not at the promise of God through unbelief, but was strong in faith, giving glory to God

~Romans 4:17, 20

There are many principles that govern the law of faith. The law of faith is to believe in the unseen. It is also a law that says to have faith enough to see a future (the invisible) and desire it. A vision will propel a desire and the rest will be set in motion.

The Power of Vision
The power of vision is the fundamental principle of the law of faith. The power of vision will create a desire and a desire will bring about an accomplishment. Therefore, your ability to be diligent, disciplined and dedicated to hard work are the law of faith.

The Power of Desire
"The desire accomplish is sweat to the soul" (Proverbs 13:19). Every desire must be rooted out of Love from the

heart. You can believe anything out of your heart. You can also believe the outcome of your future from the heart. Romans 10:10 says, ***"with the heart man believeth unto righteousness and with the mouth confession is made unto salvation."*** Practice what you preach, stand up for what you believe and live by the power of your vision. Never consider quitting as an option; quitters don't win and winners don't quit. Clement W. Stone once said, "Tell everyone what you want to do and someone will help you do it." Total commitment and persistence is the principle behind the outcome of faith. This is a fundamental principle in the law of faith. Blind your eyes and deafen your ears to criticism, conflicts and confrontation. Learn to live an offence free life. If you can operate under the love of Christ and practice advance forgiveness, nothing will move you from your place hence forth, in the name of Jesus, Amen! The law of faith demands that you live and operate in love. Romans 13:8 says, ***"owe no man nothing, but love."*** If you can plant this principles in the bottom of your heart every issue of your life will prosper, grow and increase with ease. The scripture says, from the heart comes the issues of life (Proverb 4:23). Love is a commandment (1 John 5:2, Genesis 11:6).

Briefly, let me share a few important fundamental laws of faith that will produce the outcome of faith.

The Power of Your Word
Matthew 12:36-38

"But I say unto you, that every idle word that men shall speak, they shall give account thereof in the day of Judgment. For by thy words thou shall be justified and by thy words thou shall be condemned."

Your words are living seeds, what you say determines what you get. Job 22:28 says, ***"Thou shall also decree a thing, and it shall be established unto thee; and the light shall shine upon thy ways."*** What you say will determine what you will see as well as the results you experience in life. For the outcome of your faith to favor you, you must speak what you desire to come to pass in your life. God is committed to doing that which you desire only when you speak it out. God said, in Numbers 14:28, that ***"as ye have spoken in mine ears, so will I do to you."*** This is a pre-requisite for the outcome of your faith to produce. If you can, clean up every limitation, curse, spell, evil thoughts ideas you brought upon your life; break the words which were cast against you as a curse or spell by someone who hates you or hates your whole family. Thereafter, you renew and reverse every spoken word and your future will receive a fresh start and a new beginning to overcome every challenge, battle, obstacle and mountain. In John 15:2, the bible says, ***"Now ye are clean through the***

word which I have spoken unto you." The word of God is for sanctification edification and cleansing. John 17:17 says, ***"Sanctify them through thy truth; thy word is truth."*** Your tongue is full of power, it controls the issues of your life.

James 3:5-6 says, ***"Even so the tongue is a little member and boasteth great things. Behold, how great a matter a little fire kindleth! And the tongue is a fire, a world of iniquity: so is the tongue among our members, that is defileth the whole body, and setteth on fire the course of nature, and it is on the fire of hell."*** Until you begin to say what you want, you will not see the outcome of your faith. Whatsoever you desire when you pray, believe that you receive it and you shall have it.

Learn to escape the trap of the enemy. Do not allow your words to condemn and justify the outcome of your faith. The bible says that by your word you are condemned, by your words you are justified. Proverbs 6:2 says, ***"Thou are snared with the words of thy mouth, thou art taken with the words of thy mouth."***

The third principle to the law of faith is the power of love.

The Power of Love
Romans 13:8
"Owe no man anything, but to love one another; for he that loveth another hath fulfilled the law."

Every lover is a giver. "For God so loved the world he gave His only begotten son." King Solomon loved the Lord and he and gave. The bible says that God is Love (1 John 4:8, 16). 1 Kings 3:3 says, **"And Solomon loved the Lord, walking in the statue of David his father: only he sacrifice and burnt incense in high places."** The scripture teaches that whatsoever is not faith is sin, and faith cannot work without love. For the outcome of your faith to be prosperous, you must live in Love. Galatians 5:6 states: **"but faith which worketh by love is the first and greatest commandment."** For love to function you must operate in an offense free life. To love God means to love thy brother. 1 John 3:14-16 says, **"For Love to operate you must love the Lord with no reservation."** The Psalmist said Great peace have they which love thy Law and nothing shall offend them.

In summary, in order to observe the law of faith, you must keep the law of Love. In Galatians 5:6 it says, **"but faith which worketh by love."** 1 John 4:8 reiterates that **"God is love."** 1 John 4:16 states: **"He that dwelleth in God dwell-**

eth in love and God in him." Watch what you say against yourself, others, God and Satan. Your words are seeds. In the kingdom of God, and even outside the kingdom of God, your words are seeds. You are responsible for what you say. Ignorant of the spoken word is no excuse. Numbers 14:28 (NIV) says, *"So tell them, 'As surely as I live, declares the LORD, I will do to you the very thing I heard you say."* One of principles of the <u>Your</u> future is in your words; your future is in your mouth.

The Power of Focus
Luke 9:62
"And Jesus said unto him NO man having put his hand to the plough and looking back is fit for the kingdom of God."

Focus is defined as concentrating on one thing in particular. Focus means to fix or to settle on one thing. Jesus, in this scripture, commanded us to pay attention to one specific thing. In Luke 10:42, Jesus said, *"one thing is needful and Mary has chosen that good part which shall not be taken from her."* If David had not concentrated on one thing, he (David) would have been a victim of circumstance. David said, in Psalm 27:4, *"One thing have I desired of the Lord that I will seek after, that I may dwell in the house of the Lord all the days of my life, to behold the beauty of the*

Lord and to enquire in His temple."

In order for every believer to be successful and productive in life, we must strive not only for excellence, but to forget those things which are behind. Paul said, in Philippians 3:13-14, *"but this one thing I do, forgetting those things which are behind and reaching forth unto those things which are before, I press (focus) towards the mark for the prize of the high calling of God in Christ Jesus."* It will cost you to be quiet, study and focus. 1 Thessalonians 4:11 says, *"And that ye study to be quiet and to do your own business and to work with your own hands, as we commanded you."* It takes the grace of God to be focused in all endeavors of life. Focus is crucial and fundamental towards exploiting excellence and greatness. Focus is to concentrate and place all of your attention on one thing so that you come out with successful results. The Bible says that those who compare themselves among themselves, are not wise (2 Corinthians 10:12).

The vision can be for an appointed time, but it takes focus to actualize a vision (Habakkuk 2:3). Whatever thy hand findeth to do, do it with thy might (Ecclesiastes 9:10). Learn to do well and focus in your life. Streamline your plans and purpose in life in terms of a SWOT analysis: Strengths, Weakness, Opportunities, Threats). Shortly after you do this, the gift of God will begin to flourish in your life, in Jesus' name, Amen! There is a gift of God in your life. Discover it. (1 Corinthians 7:7, 17, 20, 24). John the Baptist preached the baptism of repentance and Jonah preached judgment to the city of Nineveh. Paul said, that I may know him and the power of His resurrection. If you repent and focus your life God will do a new thing. The Lord said, *"remember ye not the former things neither consider the things of old; behold I will do a new thing; now it shall spring forth"* (Isaiah 43:18-19). If you have not been focused in any area of your life, make today your day of return. If you return, God will restore you. The outcome of your faith will be rewarding, if you begin to focus with the remaining portion of your life.

Benefits to be focus in life

1. *Success:* When you focus, it may take time, but you will succeed in the end (Habakkuk 2:3).

2. *Clarity:* Focus delivers clarity in life (Proverb 18:16, Romans 11:29, 1 Corinthians 7:7, 17, 20,24).

3. *Prosperity:* Focus generates prosperity (Joshua 1:8).

4. *Blessing:* Focus delivers generational blessings (Genesis 49:26).

5. ***Comfort:*** Focus grants comfort (Isaiah 40:1-2).

The Power of Decision
Joel 3:14
"Multitudes, multitudes in the valley of decision; for the day of the Lord is near in the valley of decision."

Decisions are powerful and crucial in the race of life. The instructions you obey will determine the future you create. I do not agree with what someone said on a TBN television program one time. They said it is direction, and not your intention, that will determine your destination. Until you choose to see your future in the scripture, your future will not feature. Your future will not feature, if you cannot see the outcome of your life today.

Do you want to make heaven? Then make an eternal decision today. If you can capture your vision through the power of your decision, it will change the playing field of your life. In every sphere of life, decisions are crucial. Men of decisions are men of responsibility. Decisions will make and break you. Your today is a product of the decisions you made yesterday. It takes the grace of God to make a noble decision. The grace of God is the power of God; it is what makes you great in the kingdom of God.

If you choose to serve God, He is determined to bless you. Joshua 24:15 says, *"choose you this day whom ye will serve."* If you begin to serve, God will begin to bless you. Until you start serving, God cannot commence to release His blessings. *"And ye shall serve the Lord thy God and he shall bless thy bread, and thy water, and I will take away sickness away from the midst of thee"* (Exodus 23:25). *"Return unto God and God will return unto you"* (Malachi 3:7). *"If ye turn unto God, God will turn unto you"* (Zechariah 1:3). Anytime you return, God is committed to restore.

Men who make decisions are men of responsibilities. Only leaders are decision makers, and leaders are learners. Receive the power of God to make noble decisions in your life, in Jesus' name. The scripture teaches that the prodigal son made a decision and said, *"I will arise and go to my father"* (Luke 15:18). Are you committed to make sincere decisions to return unto God today? Joshua 18:3 says, *"How long are ye slack to go to possess the land which the Lord God of your father hath given you?"*

Do you want to start a business? Tell everyone about it. For W. Clement Stone said "Tell everyone of what you want to do and someone will help you do it." Is your environment hindering you? He said that you are a product of your environment. Decide today and begin, nothing will restrain you, in Jesus' name (Genesis 11:6). The power of decision is embedded in the hand of God. You can fall, but you must get back up (Proverb 24:16). Job lost all, but God restored the latter end of his life. He gave him more than what he had at the beginning (Job 42:12). Paul was sent to prison, but at midnight he was released (Acts 16:26). Peter went into prison, but the angel of God broke him out (Acts 12:7). Daniel was thrown to be meat for the lions, but the angel of God safeguarded him out; the king released him the next day (Daniel 6:22). Agree and decide today that your light has come and God will grant you the grace to make it in the race of life.

To decide the outcome of your faith is your own choice. (Deuteronomy 30:19). Indecision has kept you stagnant for a long time. ***"Wherefore he said Awake thou that sleepest and arise from the dead and Christ shall give thee light"*** (Ephesians 5:14). For the outcome of your faith to be prosperous you must make noble decisions. Indecision is a destroyer of the outcome of your faith. If you do not make a decision today, time will make a decision for you. Do not allow in-decision to become a hindering force against the outcome of your faith. ***"God is not an author of confusion"*** (1 Corinthians 14:33). In-decision must be destroyed, in Jesus name, Amen.

Let us briefly look at the consequences of in-decision:

1. Confused: You will continue to be confused until you make a decision (1 Corinthians 14:33).

2. Doubt: It will imprison you and cloth you with darkness (James 1:8).

3. Uncertainty: Until you take a giant step, you will remain in mediocrity (2 Kings 7:3-10).

4. Fear: False evidence appearing real will hurt your future (Psalm 53:5, Isaiah 41:10).

5. Stagnation: This is where you will remain until you decide it is your turn for a turn around (Deuteronomy 2:3).

The Outcome of Faith Prayer

Every wicked tongue hired against me, catch FIRE, in the name of Jesus.

Any Power strengthening my problem, roast by FIRE, in the name of Jesus.

Every gathering of my adversaries, S-C-A-T-T-E-R, in the name of Jesus.

Where is the Lord God of Elijah? Arise, INCREASE MY SPEED, in the name of Jesus.

Any power assigned to steal my glory, your time is up, DIE, in the name of Jesus.

Any evil hand raised to strike me, DIE, in the name of Jesus.

Power of breakthrough, hit me with fire and speed, in the name of Jesus.

CHAPTER 4

Understanding the Power of Winning Faith

"For whatsoever is born of God overcometh the world, and this is the victory that overcometh the world, even our faith."

~ 1 John 5:4

Nothing will work for you until your carry an all-things-are-possible mentality. The outcome of your faith will not be prosperous until you develop an overcomers mentality. An overcomers mentality means believing that there is a way out of that obstacle, there is a way forward out of that battle and there is a way up, out of that challenge. There is no substitute to this requirement. Until you develop a bold and fearless mentality, you cannot be a candidate of the winning faith. The outcome of your faith is the prosperous faith and the prosperous faith is the winning faith. In Mark 9:24, Jesus said, ***"unto him if thou can believe all things are possible to him that believeth."*** The winning faith is a living force and the living force is the shield of faith that quenches all the fiery darts of the wicked (Ephesians 6:16). Until your faith is crucified with Christ, you are not worthy of the winning spirit (Galatians 2:20). It is the winning spirit that produces the winning faith, and it is the winning faith that commands supernatural results in the midst of great impossibilities.

Although the winning faith works by love, it will not be prosperous without obedience. When you obey the scripture, you create a future for yourself. The outcome of faith is engaging the word of God to enforce your desired victory. ***"Faith without works is dead"*** (James 2:20, 26). ***"If God be for us who can be against us?"*** (Romans 8:31). ***"For with God nothing shall be impossible"*** (Luke 1:37). ***"Without faith it is impossible to please God"*** (Hebrews 11:6). The faith here is the winning Spirit to conquer all obstacles, climb any mountain and defeat any challenge. The power of the winning faith here is in your action. The scripture says that by God actions are weighed (1 Samuel 2:3).

On a daily basis, you do almost everything by faith without knowing it. Why not engage the winning spirit of faith to overcome obstacles, challenges and the battles of life? The outcome of faith is a product of inner strength. You have to develop a mind-set that says it can be done. Mary said, in Luke 1:38, ***"be it unto me according to thy word."***

There is a great poem by Williams J Bennett titled:
"It can be done"

> The man who misses all the fun
> Is he who says, "it can't be done"
> In solemn pride he stands aloof
> And greets each venture with reprove.
> Had he the power he'd efface
> The history of the human race;
> We'd have no radio or motorcars;
> No streets lit by electric stars;
> No telegraph nor telephone,
> we'd linger in the age of stone
> The world sleep if things were run
> by men who say, "it can't be done"

Zig Ziglar once said, "Put all excuses aside." Remember this: you are capable! That challenge or obstacle can be crushed. You are capable; it can be done. Your challenge is not something new (Ecclesiastes 1:9-10).

I repeat the last two lines: <u>The world sleep if things were run by men who say, "it can't be done.</u>" It is the outcome of faith that has changed the world. Dr. Robert Schuller, a great preacher said, "possibility thinking is faith focused on achieving a definite goal." Without the outcome of faith there will be no innovation anywhere in the world. It is the outcome of faith that has changed men both in the kingdom of God and outside the kingdom of God.

The Power of imagination will produce the desired results. Nahum 1:9 says, *"what do ye imagine against the Lord? He will make an utter end affliction shall not rise up the second time."* The scripture says, in Genesis 11:6, says, *"and this they begin to do; and now nothing will be restrained from them, which they have imagined to do."* There is a lot of potential inside of you. You are born to be great. Job 28:3 declares that *"He setteth an end to darkness."* I decree every work of the forces of darkness has come to an end in your life, in Jesus' name, Amen!

The reason you are reading this book is because God has made up His mind to use you. Never consider the work of the enemy. Listen to me, Psalm 9:6 says, *"O thou enemy, destructions are come to a perpetual end."* Jesus said that *"the works that I do shall he do also, and greater works than these shall he do, because I go to my father."* The Power of the winning faith is hidden in God's leading (Isaiah 48:21). God cannot lead a man who does not have faith. You have to discover the gift and calling of God upon your life (Romans 11:29).

Vision is your ability to locate God's plan and purpose for

your life. Your life will remain plain until you locate God's plan. You will be battered if you do not follow God's pattern for your life. It is the gift of God that will make room and bring you before great men (Proverbs 18:16). Psalm 89:34 says, ***"My covenant will I not break nor altar the words that has gone out of my mouth."*** God is waiting for your manifestation (Romans 8:19). God is waiting for your profiting to appear to them all (1 Timothy 4:15).

It is the power of the winning faith that generates the healing faith. Healing cannot take place without the power of winning faith. The woman with the issue of blood said, ***"if I may touch but his clothes, I shall be whole"*** (Mark 5:28). James 5:15 says, ***"And the prayer of faith shall save the sick, and the Lord shall raise him up and if he hath committed sins, they shall be forgiven him."***

CHAPTER 5

Understanding the Invisible Barriers

"For a great door and effectual is opened unto me, and there are many adversaries."

~ 1 Corinthians 16:9

You are not a candidate of breakthrough until you discover your own mountain of ignorance. We must not be ignorant of the devices of the enemy. I pray that all devices of the enemy covering your illumination and understanding shatter, in the name of Jesus, Amen. Every emerged champion must wrestle and defeat a reigning champion. Until you defeat the goliath against your life, you are not entitled to the crown. Every grand battle must be fought out of faith. Through faith, David destroyed goliath. Until you discover and deal with your own goliath, it is not your turn for victory. There are mountains of obstacles, challenges and barriers that have resisted your rising. Exodus 3:19 says, *"and am sure the king of Egypt will not let you go, no, not by a mighty hand."* Until you put up a fight, you are not permitted to rise. Paul said fight the good fight of faith. Lay hold on eternal life (Timothy 6:12). Every battle in life answers to your faith. Be it done unto thee according to thy faith. Every challenge will be answered according to your faith (Matthew 9:29, Matthew 15:28). God said He has given us a mouth and a wisdom which our adversaries cannot gain say nor resist. Your faith will produce only at the level of what you say. There is power in the right word. It is important to note that the devils devices you do not deal with today will grow to become a dragon tomorrow. In Genesis 3:14 it says, ***"The Lord said unto the serpent,"*** but in Revelations 12:7, "when there was war in heaven, Michael and his angels fought against the dragon. The serpent in Genesis turned into a dragon in the book of Revelation. Therefore deal with all barriers and strongholds against you today in the name of Jesus. The bible says, in Genesis 3:14, ***"And dust shall thou eat all the days of thy life."*** Satan's food is dust! And Man was made from dust. Genesis 3:14 says, ***"for dust thou art and unto dust shall thou return."***

Understand invisible barriers and deal with the stronghold of the enemy, in Jesus' name. Spiritual strongholds must answer to the power of what you said out of faith. Say what you want to see with a strong force from your mouth (Job 6:25). How forcible are right words! Never settle for what will be. It is a lie from the pit of hell. Jesus is Lord yesterday, today and forever more.

Let us examine some invisible barriers

1. Sin: Constant repetition of sin is called iniquity. Sin will blind your mind and keep you in perpetual darkness. Sin will steal and withhold your blessings. Paul said, ***"sin shall no more have dominion over me."*** Sin will make a way seem right unto a man, but the end thereof are the ways of death. Confess your sins and release yourself from any known sin, act, guilt and condemnation. God is merciful to redeem and deliver you from the claws and jaws of invisible forces and powers of darkness waging war against your future.

2. Indecision: This is your opportunity to make up your mind. You have tarried in the valley of indecision for a very long time. Awake thou that sleepeth and arise from the dead and Christ shall give thee light. Let faith provoke you to make a noble decision today that will determine your tomorrow.

3. Past failures: If you consider your past failures you will never move forward. I want to announce to you that your past is behind you and your future is before you; that your own yesterday ended last night and the best part of your life is yet to be lived. Isaiah 43:18 says, ***"Remember ye not the former things, neither consider the things of old."*** There is a future for you. Forge those things which are behind. I see God opening a new chapter in your life, in Jesus' Name.

4. Fear: Fear is a device of the enemy to kill your faith. Fear has torment. The bible says fear not, do not be dismayed for I am with you. Fear is a trap of the enemy to keep you stagnant (Job3:25).I pray for faith to arise in you and destroy all appearance of fear inside you, in Jesus' Name, Amen. Be bold from today, in the name of Jesus, Amen!

Conclusion
2 Corinthians 13:5
"examine yourselves, whether ye be in the faith, prove your own selves."

Romans 12:3
"God hath dealth to every man the measure of faith."

You cannot finish reading this book without any touch and light from above! Gods hand has reached out to your situation, challenges and condition. Your life has received a faith inoculation. A new order of faith that produces results has come upon you. The Power of the highest has overshadow you. Begin your life a fresh by living by faith, for whatsoever that is not done by faith is sin. Believe the word of God and believe the servant of God. I see you climbing the mountains of life, in Jesus name, say Amen!

Accept spiritual responsibility. Reject the passive "God will do it" mentality and "what will be will be" attitude. Put your faith to work (James 2:20, 26). Take steps, be focused, let your actions speak hence forth. Start working towards your desired goals. The scripture says, ***"nothing is impossible to him that believe."*** Never accept assumptions. Those who lived in assumptions died of frustration and affliction. God has done His part, He is a covenant keeping God. It is now your turn to arise and shine. I pray that the mantle of the spirit of faith come upon you that you may overcome all your trials, troubles, tribulations and longsuffering, in the name of Jesus, Amen!!!

Now say these prayers!

Prayer against invisible barriers

1. Every invisible agent assigned against my life, die, in the name of Jesus.

2. Anointing for constant open heavens, fall on me now, in the name of Jesus.

3. Every power assigned to steal my blessings, I strike you with confusion, in the name of Jesus.

4. God of Isaac arise and multiply and establish me this

year, in the name of Jesus.

5. Powers ordained by heaven to make me great, arise and locate me, in the name of Jesus.

6. Every stone placed against my moving forward, scatter, in the name of Jesus.

7. Glory of God, speak for me this year, in the name of Jesus.

8. Strange enemies, assigned to afflict my life, receive violent angelic slap, in the name of Jesus.

9. I bind witchcraft covens working against my future, in the name of Jesus.

10. Witchcraft money, introduced into my business and finances, catch fire, in the name of Jesus.

11. Garments of disappointments, catch fire, in the name of Jesus.

12. My life, hear the word of the Lord, that there is a God in Israel, in the name of Jesus.

Summary

Faith is a secret mystery that can only be understood through proof. Only fools doubt proof. Even the heathen, who understands and engages the mystery of faith, prospers. Simply defined, this book, *The Outcome of Faith*, tells you the end product of faith. **The Outcome of Faith** is the guaranteed bountiful blessing and riches of God. Without faith you can not please God. Without faith, you cannot uproot and take hold of your blessings and material abundance.

Apply what is presented in this book and see how quickly God will change your situation.

About the Author

Rev Franklin N Abazie is the founding and Presiding Pastor of Miracle of God Healing Church with headquarters in Newark, New Jersey USA and a branch church in Owerri-Imo State Nigeria. He is following the footsteps of one of his mentors, Oral Roberts (Healing Evangelist) of the blessed memory. The Lord passed Oral Roberts healing mantle two days before he went to be with the Lord at age 91 into the hand of healing evangelist-Rev Franklin N Abazie in a vision.

In all his services the Power and Presence of God is present to heal all in his audience. He is an ordained man of God with a Healing Ministry reviving the healing and miracle ministry of Jesus Christ of Nazareth.

Pastor Franklin N Abazie, is called by God with a unique mandate: "THE MOMENT IS DUE TO IMPACT YOUR WORLD THROUGH THE REVIVAL OF THE HEALING & MIRACLE MINISTRY OF JESUS CHRIST OF NAZARETH I AM SENDING YOU TO RESTORE HEALTH UNTO THEE AND I WILL HEAL THEE OF THY WOUNDS. SAID THE LORD OF HOST"

He is a gifted ardent teacher of the word of God who operates also in the office of a Prophet, generating and attracting undeniable Signs & Wonders, Special Miracles and Healings, with Apostolic Fireworks of the Holy Ghost. He is the founding and presiding senior Pastor of this fast growing Healing ministry. He has written over 86 inspirational, healing and transforming books covering almost all aspect of divine healing and life. He is happily married and blessed with children.

MIRACLE OF GOD HEALING MINISTRIES

Nigeria Healing Crusade 2012
Uli, Anambra State, Nigeria

www.ingramcontent.com/pod-product-compliance
Lightning Source LLC
Chambersburg PA
CBHW020703300426
44112CB00007B/500